Cat Kisses

Sandpaper kisses
on a cheek or a chin—
that is the way
for a day to begin!

Sandpaper kisses—
a cuddle, a purr.
I have an alarm clock
that's covered with fur.

—*Bobbi Katz*

Time to Rise

A birdie with a yellow bill
Hopped upon the window sill,
Cocked his shining eye and said:
"Ain't you 'shamed, you sleepyhead!"

—*Robert Louis Stevenson*

Little

I am the sister of him
And he is my brother.
He is too little for us
To talk to each other.

So every morning I show him
My doll and my book;
But every morning he still is
Too little to look.

—*Dorothy Aldis*

Singing

Little birds sing with their beaks
In the apple trees;
But little crickets in the grass
Are singing with their knees.

—*Dorothy Aldis*

from The Blackbird

In the far corner
close by the swings,
every morning
a blackbird sings.

His bill's so yellow,
his coat's so black,
that he makes a fellow
whistle back.

—*Humbert Wolfe*

Busy Summer

Bees
make wax and honey,

Spiders,
webs of silk.

Wasps
make paper houses.

Cows
make cream and milk.

Dandelions
make pollen
for the bees to take.

Wish that I
had something
I knew how to make.

—*Aileen Fisher*

Autumn Leaves

One of the nicest beds I know
isn't a bed of soft white snow,
isn't a bed of cool green grass
after the noisy mowers pass,
isn't a bed of yellow hay
making me itch for half a day—
but autumn leaves in a pile *that* high,
deep, and smelling like fall, and dry.
That's the bed where I like to lie
and watch the flutters go by.

—*Aileen Fisher*

Haiku

A discovery!
On my frog's smooth, green belly
there sits no button.

—Yayû

The Island

They mowed the meadow down below
Our house the other day
But left a grassy island where
We still can go and play.

Right in the middle of the field
It rises green and high;
Bees swing on the clover there,
And butterflies blow by.

It seems a very far-off place
With oceans all around:
The only thing to see is sky,
And wind, the only sound.

—*Dorothy Aldis*

Open Hydrant

Water rushes up
and gushes,
cooling summer's sizzle.

In a sudden whoosh
it rushes,
not a little drizzle.

First a hush and down
it crashes,
over curbs it swishes.

Just a luscious waterfall
for
cooling city fishes.

—*Marci Ridlon*

We're Racing, Racing down the Walk

We're racing, racing down the walk,
Over the pavement and round the block.
We rumble along till the sidewalk ends—
Felicia and I and half our friends.
Our hair flies backward. It's whish and whirr!
She roars at me and I shout at her
As past the porches and garden gates
We rattle and rock
On our roller skates.

—*Phyllis McGinley*

from Rain of Leaves

It's raining big,
it's raining small,
it's raining autumn leaves
in fall.

It's raining gold
and red and brown
as autumn leaves
come raining down.

—Aileen Fisher

Brooms

On stormy days
When the wind is high,
Tall trees are brooms
Sweeping the sky.

They swish their branches
In buckets of rain
And swash and sweep it
Blue again.

—Dorothy Aldis

Dragon Smoke

Breathe and blow
white clouds
    with every puff.
It's cold today,
    cold enough
to see your breath.
Huff!
    Breathe dragon
    smoke
        today!

—Lilian Moore

The Storm

In my bed all safe and warm
I like to listen to the storm.
The thunder rumbles loud and grand—
The rain goes splash and whisper; and
The lightning is so sharp and bright
It sticks its fingers through the night.

—Dorothy Aldis

Some Things Don't
Make Any Sense at All

My mom says I'm her sugarplum.
My mom says I'm her lamb.
My mom says I'm completely perfect
Just the way I am.
My mom says I'm a super-special wonderful terrific little guy.
My mom just had another baby.
Why?

—*Judith Viorst*

My Brother

My brother is inside the sheet
That gave that awful shout.
I know because those are his feet
So brown and sticking out.

And that's his head that waggles there
And his eyes peeking through—
So I can laugh, so I don't care:
"Ha!" I say. "It's you."

—*Dorothy Aldis*

The Sugar Lady

There is an old lady who lives down the hall,
Wrinkled and gray and toothless and small.
At seven already she's up,
Going from door to door with a cup.
"Do you have any sugar?" she asks,
Although she's got more than you.
"Do you have any sugar," she asks,
Hoping you'll talk for a minute or two.

—*Frank Asch*

Growing Old

When I grow old I hope to be
As beautiful as Grandma Lee.
Her hair is soft and fluffy white.
Her eyes are blue and candle bright.
And down her cheeks are cunning piles
Of little ripples when she smiles.

—*Rose Henderson*

All Night Cats

They're out on the town, tappin' away.
They dance by the moon till the break of day.
The stars come out and they do too.
They're All Night Cats and they're waitin' for YOU!

—*Tomie dePaola*

The Secret Place

It was my secret place—
   down at the foot
   of my bed—
   under the covers.

It was very white.

I went there
   with a book, a flashlight,
   and the special pencil
   that my grandfather gave me.

To read—
    and to draw pictures
    on all that white.

It was my secret place
    for about a week—

Until my mother came
    to change the sheets.

          —Tomie dePaola

Covers

Glass covers windows
    to keep the cold away
Clouds cover the sky
    to make a rainy day

Nighttime covers
    all the things that creep
Blankets cover me
    when I'm asleep

—*Nikki Giovanni*

I see the moon,
  And the moon sees me;
God bless the moon,
  And God bless me.

—*Anonymous*

Copyright Acknowledgments

Grateful acknowledgment is made to the following for permission to reprint the selections in this book. All possible care has been taken to trace the ownership of every selection included and to make full acknowledgment for its use. If any errors have occurred, they will be corrected in subsequent editions provided notification is sent to the publisher:

Aldis, Dorothy: "Brooms," "Little," "Singing," "The Storm," from *Everything and Anything*, copyright 1925-1927, renewed 1953, © 1954, 1955 by Dorothy Aldis. "The Island," "My Brother," from *Hop, Skip and Jump!* copyright 1934, renewed © 1961 by Dorothy Aldis. Used by permission of G. P. Putnam's Sons, A Division of Penguin Young Readers Group, A Member of Penguin Group (USA) Inc., 345 Hudson Street, New York, NY 10014. All rights reserved.

Asch, Frank: "The Sugar Lady" from *City Sandwich*. Text copyright © 1978 by Frank Asch. Used by permission of HarperCollins Publishers.

dePaola, Tomie: "The Secret Place" reprinted with permission of the author from *Once Upon a Time: Celebrating the Magic of Children's Books in Honor of the 20th Anniversary of R.I.F.*, copyright © 1986 by G. P. Putnam's Sons. "All Night Cats" copyright © 2004 by Tomie dePaola.

Fisher, Aileen: "Autumn Leaves"; "Busy Summer"; "Old Man Moon"; "Rain of Leaves" from *In the Woods, In the Meadow, In the Sky*, Charles Scribners, 1965. Copyright © 1965 by Aileen Fisher. Used by permission of the Boulder Public Library Foundation as per Marian Reiner.

Giovanni, Nikki: "Covers" from *Vacation Time: Poems for Children*. Copyright © 1980 by Nikki Giovanni. Used by permission of HarperCollins Publishers.